Stories of the Sky

Tales from Three Cultures

Kim James
Illustrated by Nina Sanadze

Contents

What Are These Tales About?

People have always been curious about what we see in the sky. They have wondered about the sun, the moon, and the stars.

Today, scientists study space using tools such as telescopes. Long ago, people from different cultures made up stories or tales to explain how the sun, the moon, and the stars came to be.

The three tales in this book were told by people from three different parts of the world.

The Journey of the Sun Mother

A Tale from Australia

Long, long ago, it was dark all across the world. Nothing moved. Everything was silent.

In a cave deep under the dry ground, the Sun Mother was sleeping. She had been asleep ever since the world began. Her dreams were peaceful, and her breathing was slow.

One day, the Sun Mother gently woke up. As she opened her eyes, light like sunbeams shone from them. It lit up the dark corners of the cave.

The Sun Mother stepped out of the cave and stretched. Light from her eyes spread out over the land.

She breathed deeply and a little breeze blew across the land. "Waking up feels good," she said.

The Sun Mother began walking. As she walked, the light from her eyes grew brighter. Where the light touched the land, seeds felt heat and sprouted. Soon, there was a trail of grass, flowers, trees, and bushes growing behind her. She walked all across the land until it was covered with plants.

"All these plants will need water to stay alive," said the Sun Mother.

She went back to the cave, far below the ground. There, she found snakes sleeping deeply. She woke them up.

The snakes began slithering and sliding out of the cave. They moved across the land. As they slid along, they made streams and rivers.

The rivers gave water to the grass, flowers, trees, and bushes. Soon, fish and other water creatures came to live in the rivers.

Then the Sun Mother woke up all the other sleeping creatures. There were all kinds of animals. There were furry kangaroos and birds with feathers. There were slimy worms and scaly lizards. There were crawling insects and hopping frogs. Sleepily, the animals opened their eyes when they felt the warm light from the Sun Mother.

The animals found places to make their homes. Some climbed into the trees. Some lived on the ground. Some made holes in the sand.

The animals worked hard, finding food and raising their young. They all lived beneath the Sun Mother's light.

Time went by, and the Sun Mother saw that the animals were getting tired. She realized that if she stayed on Earth all the time, it would always be light. The animals

would have no time to rest, and neither
would she. So one day she traveled far
across the sky to the west. When she was
out of sight of the animals, she stopped.
She used clouds to make a bed and lay
down to sleep.

The animals did not know what had happened. Without the light from the Sun Mother's eyes, the world was dark again. The animals were afraid.

It seemed like a very long time before the sky began to glow once more. The Sun Mother had returned to the east. There, she was rising into the sky with her golden rays. The animals were glad—she had not left them forever! They began their daily work.

"This is a good thing," said the Sun Mother. "I will go on my journey across the sky every day. When I grow tired, I will sleep. Then the animals can rest, too."

So each day she traveled again to the west and sank down into her bed. After a while, the animals became used to her journey. They were no longer frightened when she went away at dusk. They knew

that she would always return and bring a
new morning.

And that is how the journey of the Sun
Mother brought day and night to the world.

Why the Sun and the Moon Live in the Sky

A Tale from Africa

Many long years ago, the sun and the moon were great friends. They lived together in a house on Earth.

The sun also had another great friend, the water. The sun often went to visit the water. But the water would never come to visit the sun. The sun had invited the water to visit many times, but the water always said no.

"Why don't you ask him again?" said the moon. "Surely he will come this time."

"All right, I will," said the sun.

13

But when the sun asked the water to visit, the water refused again.

"You see, I always travel with all my friends," he said. "There are so many of them that they would fill up your house. You would have nowhere to live! If you want me to visit, you will have to build a bigger house."

When the sun told the moon what the water had said, the moon replied, "Let's start building! It will be nice to have a bigger house."

So the sun and the moon built a big new house with many rooms. When it was ready, the sun spoke to the water again.

"We have built a bigger house! Please come and visit us," said the sun.

"Are you sure it will be big enough for me and all my friends?" asked the water.

"I hope so," said the sun.

When the water arrived at the new house, he called out, "Is it all right for us to come in?"

The sun called back, "Yes, please come in."

So the water began to flow into the house. All the fish and other water creatures that traveled with him came, too. They splashed across the floor. Soon the rugs were as wet as the bottom of the sea.

The moon was worried and whispered to the sun, "Are you sure there is enough room?"

"I hope so!" said the sun.

"Do you still want me to come in?" asked the water.

"Yes, of course. You are my friend," said the sun.

So the water and the water creatures streamed into the house. The rooms began to fill with water.

Soon the water had almost reached the ceiling. The sun and the moon climbed up onto the roof of the house.

"Do you still want me to come and visit you?" called the water. He had flooded the house and had almost reached the roof. The house was full of fish and other water creatures.

"Yes," said the sun and the moon. They didn't know what else to say.

"All right then, I will," said the water, pouring out onto the roof. The sun and the moon felt their feet becoming wetter and wetter.

"Oh, what can we do?" cried the moon. "We cannot tell your friend to leave. But soon there will not be anywhere for us to go!"

The sun looked up at the empty sky. "Well, we could always go and live in the sky! No one lives there but a few little stars."

"What a good idea!" replied the moon.
And they flew up into the sky, where
they have lived ever since.

The Sun, the Moon, and the Stars

A Tale from Asia

Long ago when the world began, the sky had no moon, sun, or stars. It was so low over the land that people could touch it easily. And although the sky was blue, there was very little light. There were not many living things on Earth—only a few people and some farm animals.

One husband and wife worked hard in the fields every day. They only stopped in the evenings when they came back home to eat. They were always very hungry after a long day's work.

Each night, the husband washed the rice for their supper. The wife cooked the rice and added other things to make a tasty meal.

One evening, the couple came home from the fields. The wife took off her pearl necklace and silver hair comb. She hung them on a corner of the sky that was nearby. Then she began to prepare their meal.

That night, they were going to have stew with their rice. The stew was boiling in a pot on the stove.

"Hurry with the rice, my dear," the wife said. "I am very hungry."

"I am hungry too, my dear," said the husband. "I am trying to be quick. But I keep bumping my head on the sky. It is very annoying!"

"Oh dear! What can we do?" said the wife. "This sky is so low that it gets in the way. I wish it was higher."

"So do I!" said the husband as he kept washing the rice. Then he bumped his head against the sky once again. He looked up at the sky in anger.

"Why are you so low?" he shouted. "I can't do my work properly. Why don't you just GO AWAY!"

Suddenly, the sky began to lift! The husband and wife were amazed. And as the sky lifted, it took the burning stove, the pearl necklace, and the silver hair comb with it. Up and up went the sky, until it was high above the land.

"Husband," screamed the wife, "the sky has taken our supper away!"

The pot with the stew in it had gone with the stove.

"And it has taken my beautiful pearl necklace and silver hair comb!" the wife cried.

The sky was now far above them. So were the stove, the necklace, and the hair comb. And they were beginning to change!

The husband and wife stared in wonder. As they watched, the burning stove became a huge golden sun. The comb turned into a glowing half moon. The pearl necklace broke, and the pearls scattered across the sky. They became tiny stars.

"What will we do?" sobbed the wife.

"Don't worry," said the husband. "We can buy a new stove, and a new necklace and comb. Just think how wonderful it will be not to have the sky pressing down on us! I feel better already!"

"That's good," said the wife, "because we have work to do. We must build a fire if we want to cook our supper now."

The husband and wife made a new pot of stew on a fire. The sky stayed high above them. And the sun, the moon, and the stars are still there.

Space

The stories in this book were created before scientists studied objects in space. Today, we know that the sun, moon, and stars have existed for millions of years. Here are some of the facts scientists have learned about them.

The Sun

The sun is a star—a huge ball of burning gas. It is the closest star to Earth. The sun is at the center of our solar system. Earth and other planets orbit the sun.

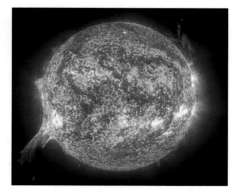

The Moon

The moon orbits Earth, just like Earth orbits the sun. We usually see the moon in the sky at night.

The surface of the moon is dusty and rocky.

The Stars

There are millions of stars in space. Most stars look tiny from Earth, but really they

are huge. Some stars are almost as big as our whole solar system!

Scientists believe there may be other stars that have planets orbiting them, just like our sun.

Think About the Stories

The stories in this book are about the sun, moon, and stars. Think about these questions.

- Which story explains why we have day and night? How does the sun affect life on Earth in this story?
- At the beginning of one story, the sun and the moon live on Earth. Why do they move to the sky?
- Think about the third story. Why do the people have a problem with the sky? How does the sky change?

To learn more about space, read the books below.

SUGGESTED READING
Windows on Literacy
The Sun
Planets in Our Solar System

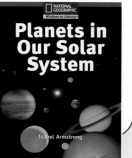